A Liar's Guide to Fishing

Ben Goode

Illustrated by
David Mecham

The Truth About Life™

Published by:
Apricot Press
Box 1611
American Fork, Utah
84003

books@apricotpress.com
www.apricotpress.com

ISBN 1-885027-26-5

Cover Design & Layout by David Mecham
Printed in the United States of America

Forward

Readers sometimes ask where I come up with this stuff. Some of you may be familiar with the story of the great composer, Handel. He told of his experience writing his opus, "The Messiah," when the heavens opened up and a choir of heavenly beings sang the music for him as he wrote it down.

So, for those who want to know, my writing experience has been something like Handel's – only without the angels. And the music I hear is generally filtering through my walls from my son's stereo.

Once I got a good start on this book, I got all excited and told some of my friends what I was working on. Some made comments like these: "So you finally got around to shamelessly trying to exploit the gift market for fishermen. You know, some awfully good "real" authors have already written some outstanding stuff on this topic. Have you no shame? Are you sure you want to do this? Wouldn't you rather be original? Must you crowd into other legitimate humor writer's territory? Next thing I know you'll be writing a golfing book."

Excuse me. Maybe I'm missing something, but I always thought that an author's success pretty much depended upon his ability to shamelessly exploit some audience. Correct me if I'm wrong, but if an author isn't shamelessly exploiting SOME group of readers, wouldn't he have to go to work doing landscaping, delivering pizzas, laying concrete or something?

So to you, my faithful, and now exploited, readers I would say, "Stand back. Ben Goode is branching into new areas. Do you know any good golf jokes?"

Ben Goode

Contents

15 Real Good Reasons To Take The Day Off And Go Fishing

Reason #1. You feel you need to do your part to help make more room in the stream or lake for water by removing fish.

Reason #2. There's a statistically significant possibility that you may see some of your customers down at the lake, so this could give you a rare opportunity to do some P.R. in an informal setting.

Reason #3. The weather today is going to be way too bad for working in the yard.

Reason #4. You need to move quickly in order to head off a nervous breakdown.

Reason #5. You want to do your part to keep the lake from being overcrowded with excess fish.

Reason #6. You need to hurry so your bait doesn't spoil.

Reason #7. You're afraid that the fish will get into trouble if you're not there to keep an eye on them.

Reason #8. It's possible that a bad accident could happen to you at work today, so, being the thoughtful person you are, you want to help your company avoid that liability.

Reason #9. Your bosses will get more done because they won't have to worry about what you're doing; they'll have one less person to supervise.

Reason #10. The therapeutic sound of running water might help your butt stop puckering.

Reason #11. You're doing important scientific research to determine how long waders last before they dissolve in stream water.

Reason #12. As long as you're fishing, you can't be robbing banks or breaking traffic laws.

Reason #13. It has been so long since you fished that if you don't go again soon, you fear you may forget how.

Reason #14. As long as you're down at the lake your family doesn't need to worry; terrorists don't know the location of your favorite spot.

Reason #15. Fishing will give you an opportunity to think through ways to increase productivity at work, to think outside the boat, as you call it.

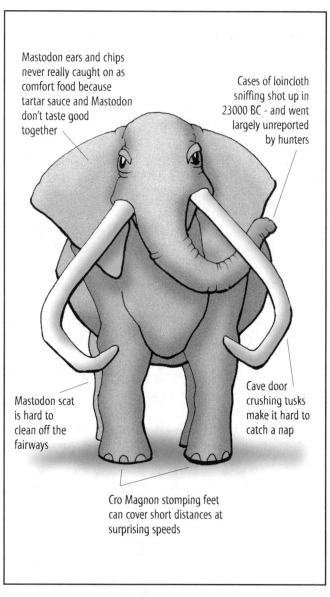

Mastodon ears and chips never really caught on as comfort food because tartar sauce and Mastodon don't taste good together

Cases of loincloth sniffing shot up in 23000 BC - and went largely unreported by hunters

Mastodon scat is hard to clean off the fairways

Cave door crushing tusks make it hard to catch a nap

Cro Magnon stomping feet can cover short distances at surprising speeds

Reasons why time spent fishing
is not deducted from a man's life...

Why do we fish?

"If God did not intend for man to fish,
why are there so many worms?"
- Socrates

If we are to understand the urge in man to fish, we must dig down through the strata of dirt and rocks and compost deep into the earth, back to primitive man to find our clues. After getting a look at the ancestors of Howard Stern, most of us conclude that if we are to learn anything of redeeming value, we must go back further still.

And so we examine Cro Magnon man. He was an early man. He hunted mastodon, so naturally, he and his wife ate mastodon. That was pretty much all they ate. They were sick and tired of mastodon. One day, primitive man's wife got fed up. (No pun intended.) In the middle of eating mastodon nuggets, she shouted, "I'm sick of mastodon. I want something else."

And so, primitive man, wanting very much to please primitive woman asked: "What exactly would you like?" And she answered, "How should I know? I've never eaten anything else."

And so primitive man thought, "I wonder how chicken eggs would taste. Giant, primitive weasels seem to like them." So primitive man found out chicken eggs weren't so bad once you got past the slimy feeling in your mouth and shells in the teeth. And so primitive man thought, "I wonder if we should try the feathers and the nest while we're at it." Watching all of this incredulously, primitive woman became nauseous.

Encouraged from his success with the eggs, man went to work sampling a long list of foods made up mostly of things he could catch: He tried bugs, snails, beetle larvae, rocks, soap, motor oil, tennis rackets, and electronic equipment. He sampled sticks, horse biscuits, tree bark, light bulbs, medical waste, and toe jam. On the one hand, man was happy because he felt he was working hard to please primitive woman; however, for the most part this all tasted pretty nasty, and deep down inside he knew he was probably wasting his time because there was no way he was ever going to talk primitive woman into eating rodent livers.

But not to be daunted, and still wanting to make points by seeming to try to please primitive woman, primitive man decided to try eating plants. This was a little better. Primitive man discovered that the leaves and roots of some plants tasted better than slugs, dirt clods, used syringes, or fur. But, unfortunately, one day, he tried some hemlock leaves. And so beginning way back then, life expectancy for man began to be statistically shorter than life expectancy for women, since primitive woman was way too smart to be putting untested biodegradable, potentially lethal material into HER mouth. Sadly, primitive husband #1 died.

So now, some time later, primitive woman remarried and once again began complaining. And her second husband, picking up where the previous primitive man left off, eventually got around to trying a bunch of non-mastodon stuff too. He tried rocks, dirt clods, and fungus. He sampled mud, furniture, and jewelry. After a few weeks of watching primitive man embarrass himself, finally, primitive woman chided, "Why don't you just try seafood?"

Primitive man paused. He was confused. The possibility of eating seafood had never occurred to him.

Cleverly, because it wasn't his idea and because he couldn't think of an easy way to catch one, he said, "that's disgusting." And they both went back to eating mastodon, and complaining until finally he had had enough. He was determined to get his lover to stop whining and to prove her wrong about the fish. And so, unbeknownst to primitive woman, primitive man began the first experiment at fishing on the sly.

He tried stabbing the fish, but that was tough with a stone knife. He tried stalking them, but getting close was hard, especially since swimming hadn't been invented yet. He tried whacking them, first with his forehead, and finally with a club, but all this did was scare the fish and get him all wet. He even took a stab at draining the stream, but he found that really sucked with only a stone straw.

So one day the primitive women were all sitting around whining about mastodon parts when one of them threw down the prehistoric gauntlet. She sarcastically suggested that the fish problem would be easy for a woman to solve. She thought for a minute and then said, "It seems to me that if you're serious, all you men need to do is put a worm on a hook along with a bubble, swivel, and a couple of sinkers, which you then tie onto the end of a line on a pole threaded through eyelets and a thousand or so lengths of nylon string wrapped around a reel."

Unfortunately, primitive man had no idea what she was talking about, but in order to maintain his self

4

respect, primitive man had no alternative but to prove primitive woman wrong. And so he went to work assembling his fishing equipment—and then getting it all tangled up, and finally getting snagged on the bottom of the lake. Instead of proving her wrong, he mostly proved himself incompetent, but he did discover one important thing: fishing was a terrific diversion from the hectic business of hunting mastodon. In spite of how aggravating fishing could be sometimes, he noticed that for this first time in his life he was totally relaxed.

And so, primitive man became a fisherman. He fished right up until the day when he was eaten by a giant cave bear. And the rest is history. From that time forth, men began to fish on the days when the boss was out of the office and they could sneak away from mastodon hunting--some days successfully, too. And primitive woman, instead of just complaining about mastodon, now had something else to complain about, and this made her happy.

And ever since that day, man has kept fishing because he genuinely wants to please his woman and because the urge to fish is infinitely stronger than the urge to eat mastodon parts. And so now, after thousands of years of this, primitive man has mutated and evolved into modern man, and that urge to fish has now mutated too and become part of modern man most likely somewhere in his lower colon, or something like that...we think.

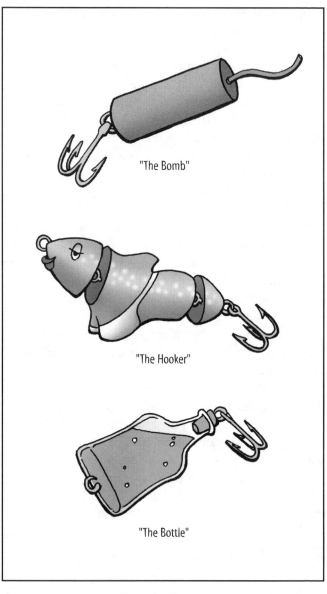

"The Bomb"

"The Hooker"

"The Bottle"

Popular Lures

Tools for fishing

"If at first you don't succeed,
have your picture taken with a fish
caught by someone who did."
- Old Norse Adage

Now that you have a little background on fishing, but before it's safe for you to really get started, we want to get all the legal and paper work out of the way. This chapter includes all the forms you will need to begin a successful career as a fisherman: Don't leave home without them.

Form Letter #1

A letter to the fish for times when they aren't biting, the direct approach. (Place this form in a bottle without a cork and toss it into the lake.)

Dear Fish:

It has come to our attention that you have stopped biting. While, in some ways we understand this since we are pretty much planning to jerk you clear out of the water by your lips or maybe remove your insides and cook you on a hot grill after you flop around on the shore for a while with a barbed hook in your throat and then hang you on a string by your gills as the life ebbs from your body. Still, we would like you to consider that it is no fun for us to sit here all day without catching anything. Therefore, we formally request that you begin biting right now.

Best wishes.

Sincerely,

The Fishermen

Form Letter #2

The sales psychology approach.

Dear Fish:

We are your friends. Relax and eat your breakfast. There is no hook inside these worms or for that matter, the cheese or salmon eggs either. You and your friends can feel absolutely safe eating all of the worms, cheese, and salmon eggs you desire, secure in the knowledge that we would never ever remove your insides and cook you on a hot grill.

Best regards.

    Sincerely,

    The Fishermen

P.S. They call us fishermen because fish are our friends. If we were trying to catch you, we would be called, "catchermen."

Form Letter #3

The Standard Non-Competition Agreement For Fishermen (this form is REQUIRED).

Be it known that whereas said fisherman knows a secret fishing spot, and whereas too many cooks spoil the broth, so to speak,

And whereas, Fisherperson "A" knows where lunkers lurk, and

Whereas Fisherperson "B" would like to catch some of the said lunkers,

And whereas the only reason said lunkers are there is because hundreds of dolts like Fisherperson "B" don't know where they are, or else they would come here so often and bring so many other fisherpersons that pretty soon there would be no more lunkers at that spot.

Now, Therefore: Fisherperson "A", herein known as _____, agrees to accompany or guide Fisherperson "B", herein known as _____, to the said spot and allow fisherperson "B" to fish there once and once only for _____ minutes beginning at precisely _____ on _____.

Fisherperson "B" hereby agrees to (1) never ever return again to said spot without the express permission of Fisherperson "A" IN WRITING, NOTARIZED, and AUTHENTICATED by 100 HIMALAYAN MONKS. And (2) refrain from disclosing the location of said spot to any other entity human or otherwise, orally, by electronic means, in person, in writing, or using any other form of communication.

Fisherperson "B" hereby pledges as collateral security all of his earthly possessions including, but not limited to, bank accounts, automobiles, real estate, stocks, bonds, other equities, spouses, children, internal body organs, pets, intellectual properties, and food.

Signed _____
(Party of the first part)

Signed _____
(Party of the second part)

Form Letter #4

The Certified Spousal Permission Slip

I,_____being of sound mind
do hereby allow_____, for whom
the soundness of his mind is irrelevant, permission to
go on a fishing expedition, which shall begin not later
than _____ and end not sooner than
_____. I also acknowledge that I
understand that in his absence there are many "honey-
do" jobs, which will probably not get done and that
while on said trip he may have some fun for which I
grant my authorization. Just leave the checkbook.

Signed_____
(Spouse)

Form Letter #5

(An authentic-looking letter from your doctor explaining to your wife why you are 2 days late getting home and why your eyes look like stewed tomatoes.)

Please excuse _____.
He has been in my constant supervised care for these
_____ days while we used intensive angler-pole-wrist-therapy to save his life and help him recover from a life-threatening attack of acute procto-craniumitis. I have released him to your custody since he is no longer contagious and seems to be recovering satisfactorily. I recommend no lawn mowing or heavy lifting for _____ years. Also, his recovery will be hastened if he is well fed and given generous sympathy.

Thank you for your patience (no pun intended).

Signed,

Doctor Pepper Zhivago MD.

Form Letter #6

(The special fishing and hunting license usually reserved for locals only.)

SPECIAL FISHING AND HUNTING LICENSE
granted to _____.

This license entitles the bearer to hunt or fish on any property, private or public, anywhere in the known world and to catch or shoot anything in the quantities of his or her choice.

Form Letter #7

(An official looking pardon from the President of the United States.)

TO WHOM IT MAY CONCERN: Be it known that

_____,

of _____ has been commissioned by the United States Government to perform top-secret research, and must be allowed to catch any number of fish of any species in any body of water in the free world. This is a matter of grave importance for our national security.

I also hereby grant him a presidential pardon from any traffic violations he may have incurred while performing his top-secret duties, and exempt him from participation in any and all diets and exercise programs. This commission expires 1/1/3004.

Regards,

President Theodore Grizwald Roosevelt

The Fisherman's Knot

 # How to fish

"Give a man a fish and he will eat for a day.
Teach a man to fish and he will
lie for a lifetime."
- Aristotle

Step 1 - Rigging up your pole

The most efficient method of rigging up a pole for most fishermen, of course, is to have Dad do it. A problem arises when, because of prior commitments, old age, or death, your dad can't be

17

there at this significant moment. In this case, you must have a strategy. It's been proven to be bad luck to rig up a pole while wearing reading glasses or bifocals. (This will probably explain why some of you have had such rotten luck fishing for so many years.) (Unless, of course, the rotten luck is planned because you are one of those who really doesn't want to catch any fish, you just go "fishing" to hide out in some place where people can't bother you.)

The first thing you must do when rigging up your pole is get a swivel out of the tackle box. A swivel is a small gold thing that bears a striking resemblance to an earwig but is more difficult to catch. Tie this swivel on to your line using a fisherman's knot (see page 16). If you don't have any swivels, you can always substitute your daughter's earring, or a spark plug from your truck[1].

Next, take out your pocketknife and cut the line just above the swivel because we forgot to tell you to thread the line through the eyelets and put on the bubble. This is because in our excitement, we almost always forget to do these things ourselves.

Repeat the process described above doing it right this time. Next, you will want to add a span (about 3 cubits) of leader-line, which is the fine line that you forgot to put into your tackle box before you left, and which you must borrow from the guy who has a string

---

[1] You can get home on only 7 cylinders—trust me.

of fish a little farther up the shore, unless, of course, he's a Jerk or forgot his, too, in which case you can go back up the shore to the place you got your feet all tangled up in some old line that was caught in the bushes and cut off a piece of that. *Make a note to get a tetanus shot when you get home just in case that rusty hook attached to that tangled line will give you lock jaw.

Step 2 - Attaching the hook

Once you have the leader line in place, it's time to attach the hook. We are going to start fishing today using cheese as bait, so we will need a treble or cheese hook. Open your tackle box again and carefully reach in. There will be a compartment in there somewhere filled with medium-sized treble hooks. That's the one we want. Next, stop jumping around like a flea on a hot pancake grill and remove the hooks from your thumb or fingers. Assuming the hooks aren't stuck deep into your thumb clear past the barbs, they will come right out. By now you have noticed that medium and small treble hooks are real hard to pick up with guy-sized hands, and since the fish probably wouldn't be biting cheese anyway, we will now switch to a worm for our bait.

Reach into your tackle box and remove a worm hook. Now, gently pull the sharp part out of your thumb and make a note to get a second tetanus shot when you get home. Repeat the process as many times as necessary. Then tie the hook onto the end of your leader using a fisherman's knot. (See page 16 again.)

Step 3 - Baiting The Hook

Now you are finally ready to apply the worm to your hook. (If you forgot to get worms, you can substitute a fish entrail, an intestinal parasite, or a piece of road kill. As you can see, fish aren't very discriminating.) But, let's assume your newfound friend a little farther down the shore remembered his worms and that he's a pretty decent guy. An entire night crawler is too big to fit onto your hook after the duct tape, besides, it probably wouldn't fit into the mouth of the fish you'll be catching anyway, so you will need to have the guy up the shore break it in half for you. If you do it yourself with all the puncture wounds you have in your fingers, you may catch something worse than lockjaw.

That was really stupid. After you pull the hook out of your thumb, carefully thread the worm onto the hook – it doesn't much matter if the point goes into his mouth or the other end; both ends of a worm are pretty much the same. Much like some houseplants and politicians, you can cut a worm into little pieces and each one will multiply into additional politicians or worms. If putting a worm onto a hook in this way makes you squeamish, use duct tape. Remember, you have two half-worms, so technically, you have at least one that you can experiment with.

There. In about the time it takes you to grow a redwood forest or map a strand of DNA, you are ready to begin fishing.

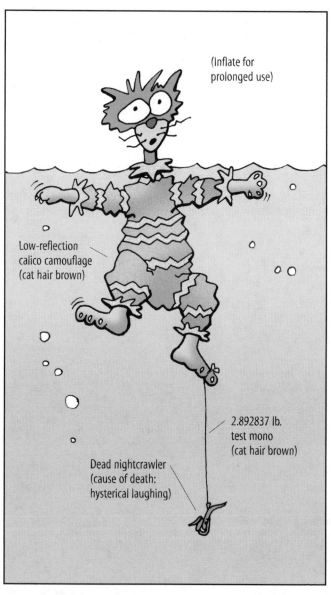

(Inflate for
prolonged use)

Low-reflection
calico camouflage
(cat hair brown)

2.892837 lb.
test mono
(cat hair brown)

Dead nightcrawler
(cause of death:
hysterical laughing)

Emergency Bubble

4 Tips for the forgetful fisherman

"If you can't run with the big dogs, so what; you can still loiter with the catfish."
- Archimedes

Sometime along the way, if not right in the middle of most fishing trips, many good fishermen realize that they have forgotten something important. Therefore, we have decided to place this chapter right in the middle of our explanations on how to fish. So that forgetting something important doesn't ruin your next fishing trip, we give you the following valuable tips.

Everyday substitutes for things you forgot or ran out of – when your friend won't let you near his tackle box...

(Although these are not perfect substitutes, most will work if you have low enough expectations)

Item: Bait
Substitute: Belly button lint, a booger, toe jam, random glands and excess lawyer body parts, dynamite, bubble gum, crawly things you find under rocks, a cat, Twinkie chunks, beef jerky.

Item: Hooks
Substitute: Explosives (they work better anyway), a hair pin, a license plate (large fish only), the dipstick from your pickup (remember to straighten it out and put it back when you're done), a cell phone antenna, your wife's earring, or daughter's nose ring. (As a bonus, if you include the nose, you also have some emergency bait.)

Item: Sinkers
Substitute: Your engine block (remember to put it back when you're done), a pebble, a cat (often takes a while to sink), a lawyer, (must put rocks in his pockets), your cell phone, your computer, a wet granola bar.

Item: Bubbles
Substitute: A seat cushion from someone's truck, dandy lions, a cat (will only float for a little while

unless inflated), a ketchup bottle with the lid on, an aluminum can with duct tape over the holes, your gas tank, your spare tire -assuming it's still inflated.

Item: Replacement fishing line
Substitute: Elastic from your underwear, dental floss, sinews from wild animals, spark plug wires (these work best if they don't come from your own truck), sinews from domesticated animals, threads from your hunting partners' buttons.

Item: Your boat or float tube
Substitute: The tires from your pickup truck lashed together (remember to put them back when you're done), your air mattress, a log, bags of garbage from the camp dumpster lashed together, a group of lawyers lashed together, a group of cat owners lashed together.

Item: Waders
Substitute: Plastic sandwich wrap, a bear's hide, random packing materials, your partner's windbreaker or jacket, an elephant's bladder.

Item: Coat or jacket
Substitute: your lambs-wool seat covers, stuffing from your beanbag chairs, otter pelts, or your dog, Sparky.

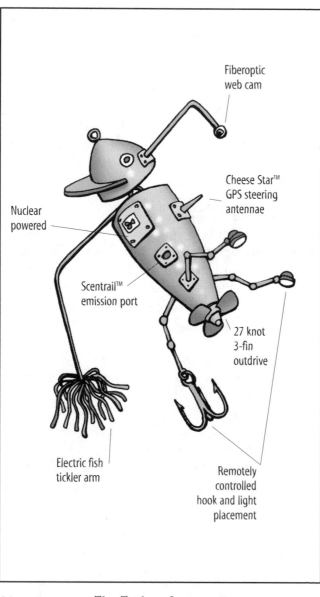

Fiberoptic
web cam

Cheese Star™
GPS steering
antennae

Nuclear
powered

Scentrail™
emission port

27 knot
3-fin
outdrive

Electric fish
tickler arm

Remotely
controlled
hook and light
placement

The Techno-Lure 2000

5 Everyone else is catching fish...

"A fish by any other name
would smell as sweet."
- Weldon Shakespeare

There are many reasons why you may not be catching fish. Fishing is a very complex sport. Catching a fish requires a plethora of things to come together just perfectly.

Equipment

Let's start with your equipment. First, you need some water, preferably some with fish in it. The following list of bodies of water will give you an idea of where you might successfully try to catch fish:

BATH TUB	(No)
SINK	(No)
PERRIER BOTTLE	(No)
PUDDLE	(No)
SEWER PIPE	(No)
LAKE	(Yes)
RIVER	(Yes)
OCEAN	(Yes)

See, you can do this. I should point out that there are some rivers and lakes, which have no fish; however, there are rarely any Perrier bottles which actually have fish. If you have been back to the same river, ocean, or bottle 20 or 30 times and have had no bites, and you never seem to notice anyone else fishing there, it could very well be that you are fishing in a body of water which has no fish.

Choosing a good spot

Unfortunately, just choosing a body of water with fish in it isn't the whole answer. If you are fishing your heart out and having no luck, it could be that you are at a perfectly good lake or ocean but you just happen to have chosen a bad spot. For example, if you are casting into the willows of the other side of the river, that (the willows) would be an example of a bad spot for catching fish.

Assuming you don't have some good tried and proven spots where you know you can catch fish, and assuming you don't have any friends who have good spots that they will share with you occasionally, you may need to find your own spot. The best way to do this is to travel around the lake or up and down the river and observe where other fisherpersons are catching lunkers. When you observe another fisherman or group of fisherpersons having a great time catching many large fish, you have found a good spot.

Clearing a good spot

The secret is to get rid of these other people so that you can have this good spot all to yourself. This can take some skill, since they were there first and are obviously having a good time, and might, therefore, be reluctant to leave.

We recommend clearing out your chosen area with bad music. All you need to drive away most other fisherpersons from your chosen spot is a vehicle that has a good sound system or a boom box, and of course some bad music. We recommend just about anything by The Beastie Boys. A few years ago we discovered how well this works when a group of fisherpersons drove the author and his party out of a perfectly good fishing spot using loud Beastie Boys music.

There are two possible drawbacks to this strategy: the first one is that you have to listen to the awful music, too, at least for a little while. We recommend earplugs. The second one is that if you mis-read the type of persons you're trying to discourage and you find that they actually LIKE the bad music, not only will this fail to drive them from your spot, but pretty soon you could find yourself fishing with a bunch of their weird friends. If this happens, before you despair, try changing the type of music to country or opera and see if that works. Or turn it up louder. Maybe they are hard of hearing or something. With luck, these could be the type of people who hate the kind of music you like.

To hurry things up and get them out of your spot even faster, you might try following the other fisherpersons around and talking to them. This works really well if you are a particularly obnoxious person, if you smell really bad or seem to have some highly contagious disease.

Choosing your bait

Some fishermen fail to catch fish because they use stupid bait. This is especially true for fishermen who are dumber than the fish. For example, a rock, earwax or yogurt would be examples of bad bait. That is because most fish don't like to eat these things. Most people don't even like these things. And even if they do, these things are hard to keep on your hook, even with duct tape. We recommend the use of

U.S.F.S. sanctioned baits such as earthworms, grasshoppers, cheeses, lawyer parts, and various lures. These can be purchased at the bait shop or lodge store nearby the body of water where you are fishing—except the lawyer parts.

Note* Some idiots have no touch when they cast. Whenever they cast, their bait goes flying or hooks a log or tree or something. Many fish are reluctant to bite a bare hook or a bare fishing line, and most fish are reluctant to take a fly while it is hooked to a tree or a log. Therefore, if you suspect you might be an idiot, you may need to use duct tape, a nail gun, or a spot welder to help keep your bait on the hook long enough for the fish to bite it or find a spot where there are no trees or other objects for your hook to snag.

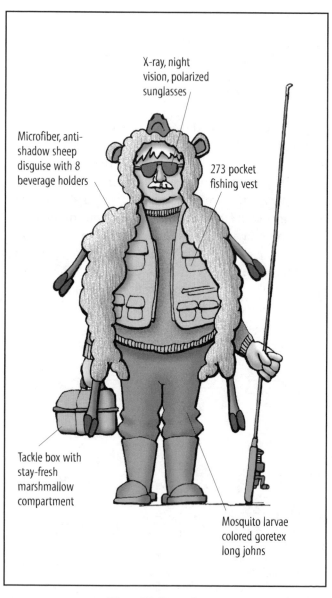

X-ray, night vision, polarized sunglasses

Microfiber, anti-shadow sheep disguise with 8 beverage holders

273 pocket fishing vest

Tackle box with stay-fresh marshmallow compartment

Mosquito larvae colored goretex long johns

New Fishing Gear

 Creative ways to get a fish to bite

"Fish now or forever hold your cheese."
- Martin Luther

When I was a kid, oftentimes we would bring a can of corn with us on fishing trips to sprinkle around in the area where we were fishing as "chum." Sometimes this was a very effective way of getting stubborn fish to bite. Because it was so much fun, and because it tended to increase the "bad" cholesterol levels in some fish, naturally most states have outlawed the practice, and so, we serious fishermen have had to come up with other ways of getting reluctant or intelligent fish to bite. Therefore, we offer a few other ways of getting the fish to bite.

Almost as good as corn, and still legal in some states, is chumming with cats in a gunnysack. Actually, there has still not been enough research done to determine if chumming with cats will really help you catch more fish, but the downside is that there is no downside. Since for many of you, cats can be hard to catch, your results can be almost as good if you chum with random lawyers or politicians, which in many places are more plentiful.

Most good fishermen know that when you stand nearby or approach the water, if you're not real sneaky, the cagey trout or bass will see your shadow and be spooked. Therefore, as you approach the lake or stream, you should configure your body so that the shadow you throw is shaped like a friendly fish, a rock outcropping, or better yet, a common deer fly.

Dynamite is an effective fish attracter. Tossing a lit stick of dynamite into a trout-filled lake virtually assures you fishing success. Unfortunately, since it is fun and so effective, naturally, it is also illegal in some places.

If you run high voltages of electricity through the water, very often, large numbers of fish will come to the top and just lie there waiting to be netted. Nearly as effective is a 50,000-gallon drum of lime Jell-O.

Sometimes, even the clothes you wear can affect fishing adversely. For example, if you fish in a bear costume fish will flee because bears are natural enemies to fish. That's why we recommend a cow or sheep costume if you're going to dress up. Avoid dressing up like little Red Riding Hood. The fish won't care, but the other fishermen may follow you home.

Since many experts say fish bite best during rain storms, you can simulate rain wherever you're fishing using a common squirt bottle. If you forget to bring one of those, but remembered to bring lots of beverages, sprinkle the "processed" beverages (beer and caffeine pollute our streams) out onto the lake to simulate rain, or in this case, acid rain. Warning: do not act drunk while other people are around.

What if you sleep in and miss the prime times when the fish are hungry and biting? You can fool them into believing it's their feeding time by snoring and brushing your teeth, or by turning on a recording of Jay Leno or Good Morning America.

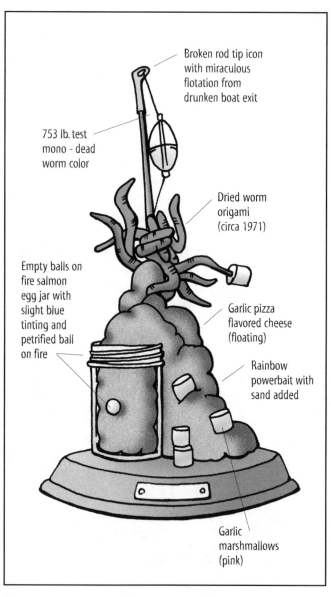

Broken rod tip icon
with miraculous
flotation from
drunken boat exit

753 lb. test
mono - dead
worm color

Dried worm
origami
(circa 1971)

Empty balls on
fire salmon
egg jar with
slight blue
tinting and
petrified ball
on fire

Garlic pizza
flavored cheese
(floating)

Rainbow
powerbait with
sand added

Garlic
marshmallows
(pink)

7 When the fish aren't biting

"A sucker is born every minute"
- Burt, caretaker at the fish hatchery

Since we all know there are some days when the fishing stars just seem to line up against you, we give you:

Some fun things to do when the fish aren't biting

Throw big rocks in the water right next to the spot where other people are fishing.

Create "bait art." Examples could include: worm sculpture, cheese mosaic, marshmallow carving, minnow jewelry, rock-roller toll painting, and mud finger painting.

Make a big tangle puzzle out of your buddies' fishing line and see how long it takes him to unscramble it.

Use a stopwatch to see how quickly you can undress and then dress again, but with your underwear on the outside this time.

Blow big bubbles using Power Bait for bubble gum.

Improvise a Yo Yo by tying worms together for the string and taping them to a bubble.

Avoid wasting the mosquito carcasses or biting flies you smash. Use them to make a huge sign on the ground that can be seen from outer space to communicate with aliens: For example your sign could say: "Do not destroy" "Friendly beings," or "Peace." If you're targeting aliens with a sense of humor try, "out to lunch," "Got Earthlings?", The intergalactic form of the symbol for handicapped parking, or "Earthlings, The Other White Meat."

Whittle a pretend fish out of a big log and then take a picture of yourself being held by it.

Do your laundry in the lake or river.

 Using your tackle boxes and fishing companions, make a ramp, and challenge the other fishermen to a contest to see who can jump his boat the farthest onto the land.

 Do some creative body piercing using spinners, pop gear and treble hooks.

 Build a kite using your fly pole as cross bar and boxer shorts as kite material. You should have plenty of fishing line to use for string.

 Set up a lemonade stand and sell lemonade to the other fishermen. You can make it by combining lake water and Velveeta cheese (use lots of sugar).

 Have a tournament with other fishermen to see which contestant can poke the most salmon eggs up his nose.

 Use your fish net to go after butterflies.

 Start a band with the other bored fishermen creatively using fishing gear as instruments.

For these same tough fishing times, here are some handy excuses for not catching any fish.

*Note: We need to mention here that one of the advantages of catch and release is that there is no evidence. You can claim anything you want. A catch and release fisherman needs no excuses. (This is one reason why some misguided catch 'em and eat 'em purists are so jealous.) Therefore, if you want to be able to say anything you want, with the added benefit of seeming to be environmentally conscious, consider catch and release.

Actually, I did catch some really nice fish, but I had to feed them to the bear so he would stop gnawing on my leg.

I spent all my time helping these Japanese tourists catch fish.

This year I decided to catch and release everything that weighs less than I do.

I worked all day to land this 200-pound bass. By the time I landed him, the two of us had bonded. I let him go out of respect.

While I was taking the monster in to have it mounted, I was attacked by an army of hunger-crazed weasels. I gamely fought them off using the fish as a weapon. By the time it was over, all that was left of my fish were some bones covered with weasel teeth marks.

40

When I went to get my string of nice fish out of the lake, a grizzly bear was eating them. I grabbed my lunch pail, attacked and fought him, and eventually chased him off, but by then there wasn't enough left of the fish to bring them home.

Regulations require that I release everything over ten pounds.

I went to pick up a few things for the fishing trip, and when I asked for "worms" apparently, the guy at the store thought I said, "ferns." Because when I got to the lake and opened up my bait box, all I had was a bunch of flowers.

I ran out of gas in my boat and had to throw all the weight out so I could paddle back to shore using my hands.

As I was walking to the shore, a tree fell over and knocked me unconscious. These guys poured medicinal alcoholic beverages all over me to try and wake me up. While they were trying to lift the tree off me, they kept giving me drinks to keep me from going into shock. Once I was good and relaxed, they were able to free me from the tree, and drag me to safety.

The forest service announced today that all the fish have gone on strike.

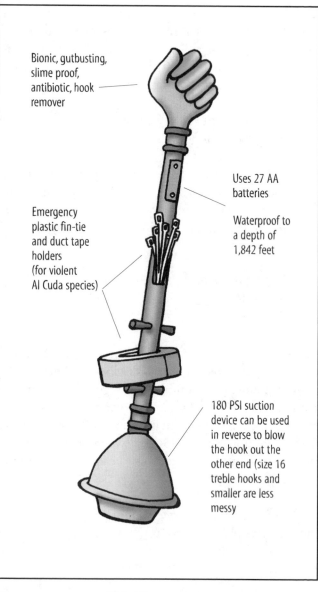

Bionic, gutbusting, slime proof, antibiotic, hook remover

Uses 27 AA batteries

Waterproof to a depth of 1,842 feet

Emergency plastic fin-tie and duct tape holders (for violent Al Cuda species)

180 PSI suction device can be used in reverse to blow the hook out the other end (size 16 treble hooks and smaller are less messy

Fish Discourager

 8 Removing the hook

"Speak softly and carry a big fish."
- Max Roosevelt

So there you are. In spite of the fact that you used duct tape to put peach yogurt onto your hook for bait, and as your line was going out you lost most of your bait to centrifugal force, some fish was stupid enough to get itself hooked. Furthering the odds, your buddies had to yell at you to come and reel it in because you weren't paying attention. Yes, in spite of all that, you got him in to the shore. Now unless you used a barbless hook and actually know what you're doing, this fish is flopping all over the shore tangling your line, spilling your Pepsi, getting all dirty and scaring the children. What do you do? You take the hook out, of course. The trick is to do it without stressing the fish and without getting slime and blood all over your hands and tenni-runners. There are at least a couple of ways this can be done.

The first way, of course, is to have someone else do it. In the event that you don't have a guide to whom you are paying thousands of dollars, you will need to find a way to trick one of your friends into handling the fish. There are two tried and proven methods of getting this done. First, you can fake an injury. Hop around and holler like you are in pain; fall down on the ground and writhe in agony begging for water – and for someone to take your fish off the hook.

Alternatively, you can convince one of your buddies that this is really one of HIS fish. When your buddy isn't looking, wrap your line around his line a couple of times and then throw the fish back into the lake. He will hear the splash, and if he's sober enough, come running to his pole, which will be wiggling with a fish on the line – sort of. Naturally, he will then reel it in, and what you hope is that in his excitement he won't notice that it's on your line until it is too late and he has already taken it off the hook.

A third method for getting your fish off the hook is to do it yourself. Good catch and release fishermen and brown bears can do it while the fish is still in the water. Keeping him in the water like this is best because if you're planning to release him he won't be nearly so traumatized, except in the case of the bear.

In the event that you are not a skilled fisherperson and you have to do it yourself, there are a few ways you can do this without getting all messy.

First, you can try dissolving the hook in solvent. Be patient. This method may take a couple of weeks. A second method that sometimes works is what professionals call the "fish hammer throw." The way this works is as follows: the fisherperson grasps the fishing line about 3 feet from the fish, twirls the fish above his head, when he gets the speed up, whacks the fish onto a tree trunk or big rock. He then repeats this process as many times as needed until the fish comes off the line. Sometimes the "fish hammer throw" method will clean the fish so you won't have to do that either.

As a last resort, some lame fisherpersons may encourage you to use what is known in the fishing profession as a "fish discourager." This is a red plastic thing that looks like it would be used by a Junior High English teacher to whack obnoxious kids on the knuckles. In my experience, discouragers are a waste of time. For one thing, it's pretty easy to tell if the fish is discouraged just by looking. Of course the fish is discouraged. How would you feel? But, using one of these to take the hook out is a lot like trying to remove the pin from a grenade using chopsticks when the grenade is buried in hamburger. It might be easier to use your teeth. If you use a discourager, figure on getting real sloppy.

Now you've caught one, what do you do? There it is in all its glory, the fish you caught. Go ahead, touch it. Take just a moment and bask in the glory. You, who have the mental capacity to diagram sentences and solve quadratic equations have succeeded in conquering an animal who lacks the intelligence to distinguish between a mosquito and Power Bait.

Once you're through basking in the glory of your accomplishment, now you must decide what to do with the fish. You have two options: turn him loose to fight another day or gut him and eat him. Choosing the first option assumes that your fish was just hooked in the lip or somewhere where the hook could easily be removed or that if he swallowed the hook and you pretty much turned the fish inside out trying to remove the hook, that you are turning him loose as food for the other fish or as a decoration of some kind or because you are fishing in a catch and release area where barbed hooks like the ones you have been using are illegal and you will get arrested. If you choose option one, you don't need any help from us.

Choosing option two assumes that you have a use for the fish as outlined in the previous chapter and requires you to now clean the fish. As the term implies, for the intellectually challenged, this means that you must remove the guts of the fish by placing his insides on the outside. There are many ways to do this, and so we are not going to take a whole bunch of our book to talk about fish guts; however, we do want to share one of the favorite ways of hassle-free fish cleaning. Dynamite! No, we don't mean this as a grammatical interjection, we mean you can use the dynamite you have left over from fishing to clean your fish. This will get it very clean. This assumes, of course, that you wanted to wear your fish, not eat it.

So, whether you remove the insides of the fish using your left over dynamite, or by using the power tools you have lying around at home, or if you choose some other method, it's a pretty simple, albeit disgusting, task.

*Note: You will notice that some fish have bones. These are annoying little things that get caught in your throat when you eat the fish; therefore, they will need to be removed. In recent years scientific technology has come up with a really slick method of removing fish bones. The same technology that airport screeners use to check the color of your underwear and develop the film in your suitcase, or that the post office uses to zap packages to kill the Anthrax, or to search for cash being sent through the mail will also atomize the bones in the nice fish you caught. Even if you don't happen to have an extra $27 million dollars to go purchase one of these machines for your tackle box, you can still debone your fish almost as easily as using restaurant workers from third world countries. All you have to do is wrap your fish up in a package and mail it to yourself. In a few days, assuming it's not the holiday season or the post office people are not on strike, it will come back to you. You can now eat your fish with full confidence that the bones are gone, because your fish went through the Anthrax screening process at the post office and has had all it's body parts containing calcium atomized. A word of caution: If you get a fish back, chow down on it, and choke on a bone, you will want to do your patriotic duty and alert the local post office. They will certainly want to know that there are loopholes in their screening process.

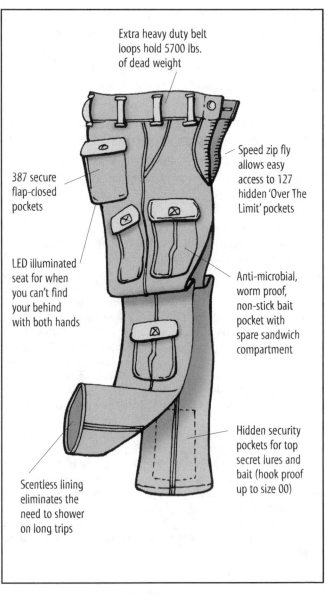

Extra heavy duty belt loops hold 5700 lbs. of dead weight

387 secure flap-closed pockets

LED illuminated seat for when you can't find your behind with both hands

Scentless lining eliminates the need to shower on long trips

Speed zip fly allows easy access to 127 hidden 'Over The Limit' pockets

Anti-microbial, worm proof, non-stick bait pocket with spare sandwich compartment

Hidden security pockets for top secret lures and bait (hook proof up to size 00)

Over The Limit™ Pants

What to do when you have exceeded your limit

9

"I fish; therefore, I fry"
- Melvin Discartes

At one time or another, we know that virtually every fisherman inadvertently forgets to read the official state proclamation, which declares fishing illegal on some particular part of some stream during June and July because the fish are spawning, and so he sees these big beautiful fish, and before you can say "watch out for that Department of Wildlife Resources officer walking this way," he has 20 or 30 nice ones lying there on the grass when the limit on the rest of the stream is 4.

Also, it's not uncommon for a fisherman to be having so much fun and concentrating so hard on the "catching" part of fishing that he forgets all about the "releasing" part and so he forgets to release a dozen or so nice fish on a catch and release only stream. And since the Department of Wildlife Resources officer now is only a little ways down stream, he could get into some real trouble releasing them now and having them swim upside down past the ranger.

Or, occasionally an otherwise responsible fisherman may, at times have trouble controlling how many fish float to the top when fishing with dynamite.

So what's a sportsman to do? Most professional anglers would advise you to just go ahead and eat the fish quickly on the spot, but since some fishermen don't enjoy Sushi, we suggest you consider the following:

Using duct tape or fishing line, attach the extra fish to your clothing. For example, a game warden would have a hard time making a case that a "trout" belt buckle wasn't legitimate, or that those lunkers taped to the front of your pants weren't just "hippie" decorations, or if you pinned a half dozen fish to your fishing hat that these weren't bait or just big lures for an exceptionally optimistic fisherman.

Hide the fish inside your clothing. For example, there is usually room inside each boot for a fish or two if you loosen your laces. Nowadays, younger fishermen can fit a whole mess of fish in the saggy part of their pants, and then they can usually fit whatever's left down their shirts, which will just make them look like well-fed, albeit unusually lumpy, anglers.

Now, once you get these fish home, what can you do with them? Here are some alternative uses for a dead fish that we've found:

Hang one above the door to ward off the evil spirits.

Use a dead fish to stop the drain in the sink.

Smoking fish can be a healthy alternative to tobacco or other carcinogens.

Judges, try using a fish as a gavel.

You can feed them to your dog – as long as he's not a fussy eater or a vegetarian.

A dead fish can be a wonderful imaginary friend for a lonely person to talk to.

Use dead fish to chum for flies or bears.

Fish make adequate bookends – for a while.

They can be used as bait to lure in a suspicious cat. A fish can often get that nervous Muffy to let down her guard and voluntarily come in closer to your dogs or coyotes.

Situated properly, a dead fish can act as a holder for your cell phone.

In tough times one could serve as a functional pillow.

For self-defense, use fish in lieu of num chucks or bollas.

With a little ingenuity and some duct tape, a couple of dead fish can be transformed into sandals or, as we prefer to call them, true "flip flops."

A fish makes a fine necklace – or, the size YOU catch, earrings.

They can be placed behind a truck or trailer to keep from rolling backwards down a hill.

A fish's schedule as recorded in his day planner

5:00 AM Wake up

5:05 AM Relieve myself in some other fish's water and go looking for something disgusting to eat.

6:10 AM Eat mosquitoes, flies, and rock-rollers being careful to ignore the worms, marshmallows, and Velveeta cheese floating all over the place.

6:15 AM Taunt the fisherman by jumping out of the water right above the spot where his worm with the salmon egg on the tip is floating.

9:15 AM Grab a bite of one last fly before heading to deeper water for an afternoon nap.

9:16 AM Be dragged to shore by the hook in my mouth as I now realize that what I thought was a fly was, in fact, bait.

9:18 - 11:30 AM Lie in the shallow water with a metal clip through my gills pondering my future.

11:31 AM Flop around on the ground waiting my turn to be gutted and cleaned.

11:33 AM Be gutted and cleaned.

11:34 - 6:30 PM Lie gutlessly in the ice chest no longer pondering the future, since I am dead.

6:31 PM Lie sizzling on the grill being turned periodically with a fork.

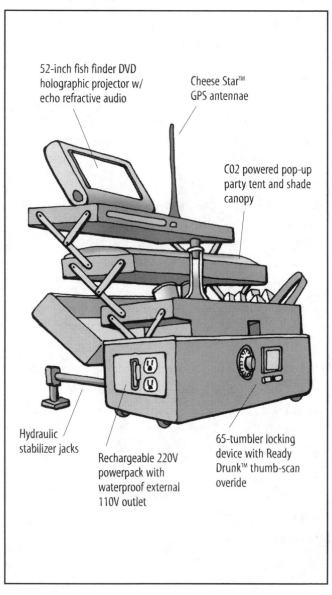

52-inch fish finder DVD holographic projector w/ echo refractive audio

Cheese Star™ GPS antennae

CO2 powered pop-up party tent and shade canopy

Hydraulic stabilizer jacks

Rechargeable 220V powerpack with waterproof external 110V outlet

65-tumbler locking device with Ready Drunk™ thumb-scan overide

10 How to choose fishing buddies

"So you can't swim with the sharks,
you can still drift with the plankton."
- Al Disraeli

I am a recovering fish-a-holic. For many years I fished alone. I would get started early in the morning and often fish until dark or even later. I fished when no one else was even around. Since I had no one to fish with, I would have gone crazy without my little imaginary weasel friend, Kevin. Kevin would go with me in the car and keep me company during those long drives. He told me lame jokes during the long dry spells when the fish weren't biting, and he gave me someone to blame when I was late getting home.

Many of you don't have a Kevin, so you can't know how much more gratifying, fishing can be when combined with good companionship. The question on many of your minds is, "Is he nuts?" And while some of you have other questions, too, questions like, "Does an imaginary fishing buddy count as a real fishing buddy?" "Do I have to show a fishing buddy my good spots?" "Does he know any?"

Rather than answer these questions, it's probably best that I deal with the other possible question instead, which is: "Where can I find some real fishing buddies, some good fishing buddies, or some real, good fishing buddies?"

Now days, there are many services on the internet, along with web sites designed to help people donate to the political party of their choice. But, since many of you don't have a political party of choice – in fact, if you did have YOUR choice, it would be to get rid of both the major political parties and replace them with Krispy Kreme Donuts, we're going to stick to fishing – and finding friends.

Some of the most frequently visited sites on the internet today are ones pretending to help people find companionship and of course, to separate them from their money – so-called matchmaker sites. These are the ones which show pictures of beautiful, sexy models, who are the last people on earth who would ever need to use a lousy web site like that to find companionship, who are being paid big bucks to act like they are common homely people who don't know how to find other beautiful models who also don't need a site like that to find companionship. These sites are of course really clogged with mostly desperate, and unattractive males who are hoping to hook up with models like the ones in the ads, the ones who can date actual hot-looking guys any time they want to, and who don't need a service like that to meet them. In other words, they would make great fishing buddies.

Most of these guys would be happy hooking up with anybody, even someone significantly less attractive than the models in the ads. In other words, instead of out-of-reach hot models, there is a good chance they might settle for good fishing buddies instead. I'll bet you can probably find tons of fishing buddies on sites like this. And after they get over their anger toward you for posing as a beautiful model, some will no doubt turn out to actually be pretty cool, albeit unattractive fishing buddy type guys with whom you can have loads of fun.

Unfortunately, while there are some legitimate matchmaking sites on the internet that will only rip off your hard earned money, there are also many many sites made by and for sick-o deviant perverts, to help them find unsuspecting people upon whom they can prey. So, as you can see, when you go to look for fishing buddies you need to be careful and avoid the sites that will just take your money.

For those of you who don't want sick-o-deviant fishing buddies, and we know there are some of you out there, there are a few other options besides dating web sites. For example, if you are so broke you can't buy worms and have no transportation, you can go to the web site like the ones that recommend doctors or legal professionals. If you find a doctor there who fishes and he becomes your buddy, he will probably have enough money to pick up the tab for everything from bait to your daughter's wedding cake.

Some of you may want to choose your older kids as fishing buddies to give you a shot at recovering some of the money they filched off you time and time again as they were growing up. You may not even need to use the internet to contact them. Many will pick up the telephone when you call – as long as you don't want to talk about the money. And, if you whine about being broke, some will even drive you to your fishing hole, assuming they have a job.

If you have younger, unmarried children or teenagers and you want to try to get THEM to be your fishing buddies, you will need to make a little more effort. You will need to use subterfuge. Sadly, they most likely will not willingly become your fishing buddies. We recommend that you surf on over to their favorite chat room or web site, (Close your eyes and try not to look at the racy pictures or listen to the awful music.) or better yet, e-mail your child and pretend you're a predator sick-o. If you send an e-mail wherein you act like a pervert, they will get right back to you faster than a lawyer in a prospective discrimination case, faster than a politician getting back to a rich donor.

While your teenage kids most likely won't be receptive to being your fishing buddy once he or she figures out what's going on, regardless of your sick e-mail, you will at least have accomplished something in the process of contacting them on the World Wide Web. Technically, this whole process can count as communication between you and your teen, and it will therefore improve nationwide statistics on parent-child communications, which are really low these days, in case you hadn't heard.

Of course, as was my case, if nobody wants to be your fishing buddy, and you are determined to fish, you can always find an imaginary friend fishing buddy like Kevin to keep you sane. Or something.

Prop Gear

11 Fishing tips

"Fish now or forever hold your cheese."
- A line from a little known early Shakespearean play entitled, "Fishlet"

(which was the only Shakespearean play extant which was a flop – no pun intended.)

The following is a plethora of great tips and suggestions, that can make your fishing experience more memorable from our gaggle of great fisherpersons.

Biting flies and mosquitoes a pain? Most anglers can achieve a statistically significant reduction in insect bites by spraying their fishing partners with sugar water as a distraction. As a side benefit, this technique will also help to keep you safe from bears.

Love fresh-cooked fish but forgot your grill and frying pan? The muffler or manifold on your pickup truck works just about as well and as an added benefit, no one expects you to clean up afterward.

Instead of using your good knife to clean your fish, announce that you forgot yours and ask to borrow the knife of a friend. This way you won't have fish guts on your knife tonight when you're cutting your steak.

Since puncture wounds can cause dangerous, life-threatening infections, whenever you're tying a treble hook onto your line and some idiot walks by and gets tangled up in your line setting the hook in one of your tender body parts, be sure the wound you make in said idiot is not a puncture wound, or if it is, either make sure he gets a tetanus or gamma globulin shot, or else, cut the wound open and let it bleed freely to clean it out. Most imbeciles will be contented if you remind them that this blood letting is being done for their own good.

In areas where fish entrails can't be tossed carelessly into the stream or lake, try tying them on to the antenna of your pickup truck. Once they dry, you will be surprised how many people will be wondering how they can get a set to improve their own radio reception.

On the days when you shear off your propeller and don't have a spare, many fishermen are not aware that they can substitute common pop gear for the prop. The boat won't go very fast, but while you're limping back to the dock, you might catch another fish.

For the times when you get to your favorite spot and realize you forgot your hat and sunscreen, some fishermen have successfully applied 1/8 inch of Garlic Power Bait to their bald heads. As an added benefit, this will also control vampires.

To avoid getting all upset and stressed out because you spend the entire fishing trip trying to untangle and re-rig your kids' poles every two minutes, as they are incapable of walking 15 feet back to the shore after you get them fixed up without making a tangled mess, scramble or tangle your child's fishing pole hopelessly before you leave. Now, when you spend the whole trip working to unscramble your kid's pole it won't be such a bummer, because that's what you fully expected to do. If you really want to give your son or daughter a true-to-life fishing experience, give them YOUR pole to fish with, and when they get it all tangled up, they can come and sit by you and work on untangling YOUR pole. Sitting side-by-side, untangling each other's poles will create a pretty cool bonding experience plus give you the satisfaction of knowing that your kids are developing another life skill.

You all know how annoying it can be to have your bagel or jam sandwich get soggy because the ice in the cooler melted, or because you inadvertently left it on the floor of the boat. To keep your sandwich dry in tough conditions, simply wrap it in a layer of duct tape.

While we're on the subject of duct tape, if you get frustrated because your fishing line keeps snagging on rocks, branches, or moss, try wrapping a piece of duct tape around each of the barbs on your hook to keep them from hooking all those unwanted objects.

During the off-season keep your fishing skills sharp. You can practice casting in your living room using a weight with no hook or barb on it – unless your wife has cats – in which case leave the barbed hooks on because Muffy will enjoy playing with the lure. Keep your reflexes sharp as you tease her by using the same action you would use to tease a trout, except, Muffy will benefit from the challenge of chasing a REAL barbed treble hook. Reward yourself with a bite of jerky every time you snag Muffy. (The best time to practice these skills is while your wife is gone and you're tending the kids.)

Things fish could be pondering:

1. Why does everything I eat look so disgusting?

2. If, all of a sudden, I stop eating disgusting stuff, where would I find something else and what would that be?

3. In the big scheme of things, will it make any difference if I wind up as the main entree' in a fancy restaurant or as cat food?

4. Why is it I never get to move up on the food chain? (Exactly where is this food chain? Can I see it?)

5. When all these other fish go to the bathroom, where does it all go?

6. If I grew opposable thumbs, what would I do with them?

7. Which is worse: having my lips ripped off a couple of times a week or being eaten?

8. Why is it that when fish die they usually float belly up, yet most other things sink to the bottom?

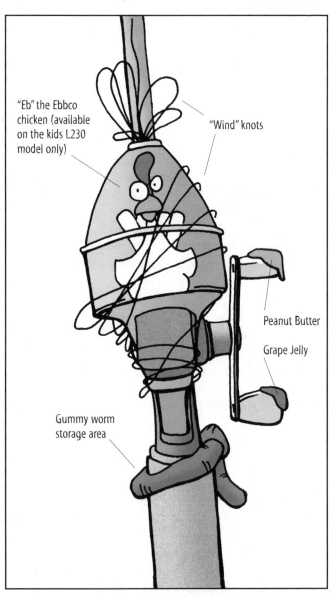

Typical Juvenile Fishing Gear

12 Taking kids fishing

"A rolling stone has gathered no moss because it was probably tossed into the water by one of your kids who is goofing around upstream."
- Norwegian Axiom

Taking a child or grand child fishing can be one of life's great experiences. A cool fishing trip can make memories that last a lifetime. Unfortunately, however, a lifetime for many old people can be pretty short, and since many old people have rotten memories anyway, making memories will be pretty much a waste of time. So instead of working on the memories, we're going to concentrate on having some fun and catching some fish. But first, we need to lay a little groundwork so the kids don't drive you nuts. Here are some suggestions to help life with kids go more smoothly, fishing and otherwise.

A few suggestions

One of the main reasons why old people don't enjoy taking kids fishing is because they're idiots. Sadly, sometimes the kids are, too. Therefore, we want to start with a few general parenting suggestions.

Some parents have a hard time getting children, especially teenagers, to do household jobs, practice piano, clean their rooms, and so on. This is not as tough as it seems. Psychologists and many Neo-Nazis have found that making a child's participation in fun activities like fishing or breathing contingent upon getting jobs done will act as an incentive. Unfortunately, fishing won't be much of an incentive if the kids don't want to go fishing in the first place. If the kid thinks that fishing with Dad is stupid and Dad refuses to let him go fishing until he cleans his room, Junior will think, "Great! If I DON'T clean my room I get to stay home and sleep or look at forbidden stuff on the internet while everybody else is gone."

As you can see, the key here is to deny a privilege from the kid that really matters. For example, the wife and I used to have a rule at our house that, until each child finished his or her homework, practiced piano, and finished all household jobs after school he or she was not allowed to go to the bathroom. We found this to be highly motivational for our children. Some of our readers have found it helpful to deny their unmotivated children food and water, air, deodorant, feminine hygiene products, anti-venom, and pain medication. And of course, some swear by the tried and true practice of locking the child in the study and forcing him to listen to classical music or Barry Manilow.

Time to go fishing

OK, let's say it's now time to go fishing; the Suburban is filled with gas, food, drink, bedding and bait. Don't forget to grab the old battery powered electric carving knife out of the drawer so you can use it to filet the fish you catch – and also to sneak up behind your teen and, cut the tissue which connects her to her best friend at the hip where they have been joined for the past two years. I don't, however, recommend this technique on teens who share a common brain. After you have separated them, scream loudly and run after the recently separated friend waving the electric knife wildly. This may discourage him or her from tagging along on your family fishing trip. It will sometimes even discourage him or her from returning to your house, but probably not.

Now that your child or grandchild is properly motivated, if you still want to, you can go fishing. Get ready to leave by luring the teen into the suburban using a piece of pizza, a bag of chips, a new video game cartridge, or a new model of cell phone. Once he or she is in the car, lock the doors and drive off quickly. Now, as long as you can keep the car moving fast enough that she can't jump out, you have a chance to talk to your teen one on one. Unfortunately, since by the time you get your car up to freeway speed, your teen will have on her headphones and will be text messaging her friend on her new cell phone, and since he or she only has half a brain left after the surgery, he or she won't listen to anything you say, but at least ONE of you will be having a marvelous time communicating and bonding.

When you arrive at the lake, the fun begins. Out of appreciation for all of your sacrifices over the years, your teen will make every effort to make fishing a great experience for both of you by lounging around looking terminally bored and asking how long you're making him stay. Don't worry about responding with words; instead, you may want to respond with the universal language of "tough love." Tough love occurs when you get sick and tired of hearing your kid whine about doing boring stuff like fishing and so you playfully take the fish you recently caught off the hook and use it to whack him over the head or jam it into his mouth. Not only does this count as communication with your child or grandchild but it will certainly make a memory.

What is a fish?

For centuries poets have eloquently described fish and their feelings toward them in song and poem. One only has to hear the song, "Fish Kiss" by Martina McBride to understand what warm feelings many people have toward their fish. We have fish filets, fish handshakes, fishy excuses, fish card games, fish food, fish eyes, smoked salmon, fish rapp, fish perfume, and Rodney Dangerfield. Fish are a vital part of our lives in nearly every way. In spite of all this fish familiarity, I know that many of my readers who struggle to recognize a fish when they see one, or don't know what to do with one when they get one. For you we offer: What is a fish? You can get an idea from the following table.

Cat	No	Onion	No
Rock	No	Perch	Yes
Guppy	Yes	Toaster	No
Musk Ox	No	Trout	Yes
Dolphin*	Yes/No	Shark	Yes
Lawyer	No	Piano	No
Minnow	Yes	Sturgeon	Maybe

*Some of you guessed right away that this is a trick question. The dolphin is really part of the rodent family. You can tell by his prehensile tail and dangling participles.

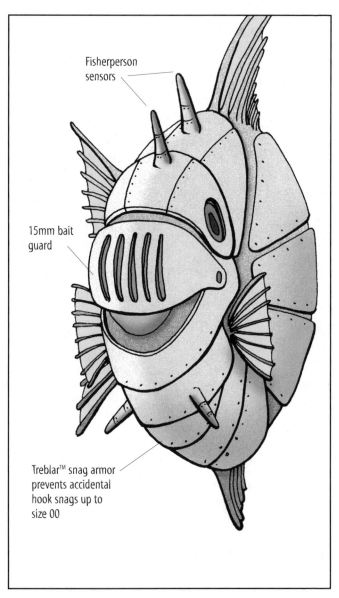

Fisherperson sensors

15mm bait guard

Treblar™ snag armor prevents accidental hook snags up to size 00

The Bionic Fish

Ben Goode

13 When does a fish count?

"When the fishing gets tough, the tough call in
sick and stay at it an extra day."
- From the Poor Fisherman's Almanac

It had been a disappointing trip. For two days we had
been fishing at one of the finest and most beautiful
spots in the West: Ferron Reservoir. But for some
reason the fish just weren't biting. My dad had tried
worms, cheese, and salmon eggs; he had tried various
dry flies, spinners, and dragging a wet fly behind a
bubble; he had tried everything in his oversized tackle
box, and even resorted to the old family curse, all with
no luck. So, after some fishermen warned us the

73

fishing there was lousy, we decided to move to nearby Willow Lake because we knew they were probably lying.

Everyone in our extended family understood that when it came to fishing, Dad was unskunkable. For as long as anyone could remember, he had always caught fish. He caught fish when no one else did. He had caught fish when they weren't hungry, when the time of day was wrong, when the fish had headaches, when they weren't in the mood, even where there were supposed to be no fish at all.

Today, however, Dad was facing his moment of truth. He knew his reputation was at stake. 40 years of perceived invincibility were on the line. With only an hour and a half to go before we had to leave for the drive home, he was now ready to resort to desperate measures. Never one to panic, but knowing that time to preserve his reputation was fading fast, Dad determined to make one final super-human effort to catch at least one fish. With the skill of a master artist, he made sure there was just the right amount of water in his bubble, sculpted a night crawler onto one #7 hook, and slid a salmon egg onto the tip for color; on the other hook he molded a perfect-sized gob of garlic-flavored cheese. Next, he lovingly soaked both hooks in the icy water and made a perfect cast straight to the spot where he knew Old Smokey lurked. Plop!

Wanting to do everything within his power to increase his odds and figuring that those odds were better if he could get some terrified fish to come back to this side of the lake, he sprang into action. With a Terminator-like look of pure business on his face, he moved to chase me and my 12-year-old cousin, Ray, into the trees hoping that if we stayed there we would be too far away to keep throwing huge boulders into the water and scaring the fish. We had been experimenting to see who could make the biggest splash, having given up fishing two days earlier, since the fish weren't biting--there are lots of other terrific things for boys to do up at the reservoir.

As Ray and I ran into the trees we glanced over our shoulders with looks of pretended terror on our faces. Normally, we would have known that Dad was only goofing around, but today we sensed things were different. As we watched and dodged, we could tell that Dad meant business. The all-too familiar "stressed parent tension" was in the air; we could even feel a little bit of anger and frustration being vented in our direction, and, with our carefree youthful perception, we also sensed that while his attention was focused on us, back on the shore Dad's pole was bending and flipping like an electrically charged orchestra conductor's wand.

In football, a good defensive back doesn't need to watch the quarterback all the time. He knows he can focus his attention on the receiver he is defending; the receiver's eyes will tell him when a ball is being thrown in his direction. Then, he can use all of his strength and energy to run with the receiver. On this particular day, I discovered that some well-trained fishermen have similar skills. My dad, while chasing us into the woods, seemed to notice in our eyes that we were watching something happen behind him. Without breaking stride, he planted his foot and made a remarkable athletic move to change directions, (for a 40-year-old guy). And without losing momentum, he shot back 180 degrees toward the shoreline and his now wildly bobbing pole.

When Dad was just a few short yards from the shore, his pole made one final super-large bob, leaped from the stick upon which it was leaning, and plunged, like a very skinny walrus fleeing a polar bear, into the wind-capped waters of Willow Lake...and then disappeared.

Never one to panic, keeping his composure, Dad began to pace wildly up and down the shore as Ray and I peeped out from behind a protective clump of aspen saplings. After a few moments, Dad's rate of pacing began to slow. Eventually he stopped moving altogether and stood, shoulders drooping, staring in the direction his pole had gone plunging into the water. He seemed deep in thought.

Timidly, warily at first, like a doe checking a clearing for safety before inviting her fawn to proceed, Ray and I began to come out from behind our tree. We moved ever so cautiously down to the shore hoping to get some redemption by giving Dad a little sympathy in his hour of need. When we were a couple yards from him, we saw his shoulders straighten. He began pointing in an animated way toward the middle of the lake. There, about 50 yards out from shore, I witnessed the biggest rainbow trout I had ever seen begin to roll as though it was tangled on something. It looked to me like the kind of trout that would have the strength to pull Dad's pole, hook, line, and sinker into the lake. This HAD to be Old Smokey.

Once again, Dad sprang into action, and before I knew it, Ray and I were stripped down to our underwear and were helping Dad push a large log into the lake. The plan was for us two boys to float on the log out a few yards toward the middle of the lake, snag the line onto which the monster fish was hooked, and drag it back into shore before we froze to death or Dad got arrested for child abuse. Hopefully, on one end would be Dad's pole and on the other end Old Smokey.

We gamely paddled out as far as we could. Unfortunately, as far as we could was only six feet, because in considerably less time than it takes a lizard to cross a hot rock, we found out that the water was colder than the north side of a southbound penguin, colder than an air conditioned igloo. It was cold enough to turn two boys into blueberry popsicles faster than you can inhale a gnat. As me 'n' Ray slid into the water, it felt as though our skin was being attacked by a thousand very cold pins. We sucked in our breath, and couldn't let it out to holler. We became highly motivated to get out of that water.

We had given it our best shot. Rescuing Dad's pole had seemed a great adventure, but in that glacier-fed lake, we didn't have enough cellulite insulation to keep our body temperatures from approaching the temperature of deep space, from getting real close to that of a weasel in liquid nitrogen. Dad and Mom lifted us shaking from the frigid water, wrapped us up in quilts, and sat us shivering by the fire.

In the brief interval before we had to head home, other fishermen were brought in to council, the forest ranger came by with a very large treble hook and tried dragging the bottom in an attempt to snag the pole. It was no use. After a few minutes, the great fish ceased rolling on the surface of the lake. The pole and Old Smokey were lost from sight. The drama was over.

Now, 40 very odd years later, I figure that fish is probably still swimming around dragging my dad's pole and line. And I am left to ponder one of life's important questions, namely: If a fisherman hooks a fish but doesn't actually land him, does it still count for not being skunked? What if he has witnesses?

Fishing technology we'd like to see

Fish finders, radar, sensors, guides who bait your hook and clean your fish for you, and the Coast Guard all combine to make today's fishing experience much more successful today than it was for anglers only a few years ago. Yet, even with all of that, there is still fishing technology which could benefit man. We've thought up a whole bunch of stuff we'd like to take with us on our next fishing trip.

-A fish appetite stimulator which would make the fish hungry at the times of the day when YOU want to fish, instead of at 4:00 A.M.

-A self-rigging pole, and its cousins, the self-baiting hook and the self-cleaning fish.

-An electronic fish corral to get 'em all into one spot.

-An automated de-snagger, or a snagless lake or stream.

-An all-digital fishing apparatus, which would let a person fish on-line using his or her mouse.

-A medication you could pour into the water, which would increase the size of the fish until they are as big as your stories.

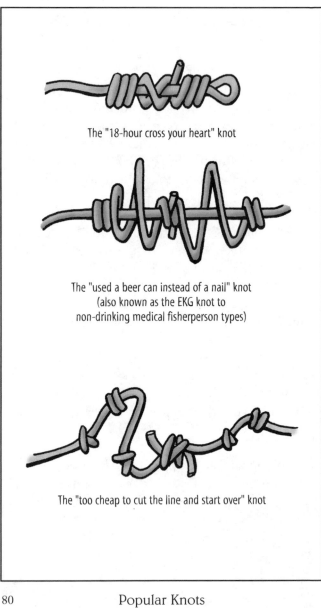

The "18-hour cross your heart" knot

The "used a beer can instead of a nail" knot
(also known as the EKG knot to
non-drinking medical fisherperson types)

The "too cheap to cut the line and start over" knot

Popular Knots

14 Measuring success

"Old fishermen don't die, they just
get tangled up in their flies."
    - From a faded, Montana bumper sticker

We were determined to catch fish. Uncle Don, my
cousin, Ray, me and my Dad set off from Grandma's
house before dawn one morning for a three-day stay
up at the reservoir. We all had a look of grim
determination on our faces, except Ray and I. (We
had the looks of slightly clueless boys, with peanut
butter and grape jelly on our faces.)

We got to the lake at mid morning, so Dad and Uncle Don decided a late breakfast would be good. Since the two of us boys had been snacking in the car on Reeses Peanut Butter Cups, string cheese, vanilla wafers, potato chips, twinkies, Cheetos, apples, Orange Crush, and beef jerky, We weren't as hungry as Dad and Uncle Don were, so, while they set to work firing up the butane cooking stove, we headed down to the lake to try and find some action so no time would be wasted. "Stay out of the water!" shouted both dads at the same time, "Breakfast will be ready in half-an-hour."

As we weaved our way down through the willows toward the water, there was a tingling of adventure in the air. The closer we got to the water, the greater the tension became, until, as we approached the shore we could hear Jaws-type music playing.

And then it happened: There, lurking right against a two hundred year old white fir was the most amazing hiking stick I had ever seen. Its twisted and gnarled beauty practically took my breath away. I guessed it must have been the staff of a wizard used to fight demons and dragons. He doubtless had inadvertently set it down to rig up his fishing pole and then forgot about it.

I cautiously looked around scanning the thick woods in every direction for the stick's owner. The last thing I wanted was to be drawn into the vortex of some wizard's duel or to be turned into an intestinal parasite or something worse. Satisfied the stick's owner was nowhere around, I leaned toward the stick. Before I could pick it up, however, Ray grabbed it and shouted, "Hey! Look at this cool walking stick!" Slightly crestfallen, I settled for a non-enchanted, un-wizard-like, pretty much generic quakie branch lying a little farther down the trail. We continued to the lake dragging our walking sticks.

Down at the shore, about twenty yards out, a beaver swam lazily, birds were chirping, mosquitoes were feeding, and fish were jumping – and then at roughly the same instant, we both saw it: another amazing find, an incredible, extraordinary, rare, partially submerged driftwood log. It had large knots on it, the bark was gone, and it was hung up in the mud.

"I wonder if it would float?" mused Ray, reading my mind.

Using every ounce of our strength, we both set to work to dislodge the log from its place on the shoreline and find out. Trying to stay out of the water so the dads wouldn't get mad, we discovered that if we both laid down in the four inches of water and mud next to the log, and pushed as hard as we could with our feet, we could get it to move ever so slowly – and the tops of our heads would stay dry.

After 10 minutes of grunting, the mammoth log finally broke free of the shore. Great! It floated nearly above the water, no, better yet, like a sinister

German submarine it drifted just below the surface. In a panic, we both dove for the log, fearing it would drift away. Unfortunately, this caused just a little bit of water to splash onto the tops of our heads, but we considered that a minor inconvenience since we had saved the log.

Precisely at our moment of triumph, we heard the voices of our dad's calling us to come to breakfast. So, again, trying our best to stay out of the water, we splashed around to the deep side of the log where it was no more than chest deep, and using all our strength, pushed it back into shore pretty much the way we found it in the first place. And then we slogged back up to camp, tingling with excitement to get back to our treasure.

Oddly, our dads weren't tingling with all that much excitement about our log, and they didn't feel that by keeping some of the top of our heads somewhat dry placed us in strict compliance with their instructions to stay out of the water, so we endured a brief clarifying lecture, changed our clothes, and humored our dads by going fishing. If I remember right, it seems like we caught some fish.

When Dad and Uncle Don finally brought the boat back to the floating pier, Ray and I bolted for the shoreline to go check on the log, explaining to the dads how important this was. After a second look, we were both simultaneously inspired to develop the log by expanding it into a raft like Tom Sawyer and Huck

Finn. So we set to work like two young, toothless, beavers building a seaworthy craft. We worked feverishly, like desperate rats burrowing for their lives in a diminishing air supply – Ok, maybe that's a little dramatic, but we probably did bear some similarities to the rodents. And so we fell into a routine. We would go get something to eat, fish with our dads, run off to work on the raft, go with the dads, catch a few fish, eat, fish, build, and so on.

By noon on the second day, the craft was ready for her maiden voyage. We christened her "The Queen Mary" on account of her extraordinary size. Since we didn't have a saw, in fact we didn't have any tools, we had been forced to build our ship using driftwood logs pretty much as God made them, and since he made them trees, what we wound up doing was piling a bunch of water logged trees one on top of the other in such a way that when we climbed on top of them, while they would sink another three or four inches under the surface of the water, sometimes they wouldn't come completely apart. We now had our own fishing craft, and we took to fishing with great earnestness from the decks of the Queen Mary.

Unfortunately, when we were fishing from the decks of the Queen Mary, since we had to work so hard to stay on top of her, since she tended to roll and shift, and since we had to use our walking sticks as poles to move her along, we didn't have much time to untangle our poles and reels or put bait on our hooks, so I don't remember catching any actual fish from the decks of the Queen Mary. However, in addition to rebuilding, and maintaining our craft, we also did quite a bit of fishing by hooking the pole to a limb on one of the logs on the poop deck and letting her drag along all tangled up behind us – at least until Ray let his pole slide into the water and get lost when he wasn't paying attention.

Eventually, we poled the ship all the way around the lake to the docks and tied her up standing in ankle-deep water. At the dock were a group of fishermen who lacked vision. They got mad because the Queen Mary was in the way and they couldn't get their boat out. We wondered if they would show this kind of impatience toward the captains of a luxury cruiser or aircraft carrier. We thought it sad that they couldn't fully appreciate the beauty of our creation.

So the Queen Mary met her demise after one brief day of being polled around the lake by some mighty fine sailors with walking sticks. She was disrespectfully torn apart and thrown onto the shore to be cut up as firewood. But during that one brief day, she accomplished more than most piles of inanimate dead weight do in an entire lifetime. She participated in the creation of cool memories for two boys, which will roll along for decades like out-of-focus sixteen-millimeter film with progressively longer sections being edited out from time to time as memories fade. So, on the way home we debated about whether or not we could consider this fishing trip a success based largely upon the number of fish we caught.

Glossary

ANGLER: Noun: The intense emotion you feel after you have taken 15 minutes rigging up your line and you lose the whole set up to a snag on your first cast.

AUGER: Noun: The sound a frozen ice fisherman makes as he tries to call for help when his face is frozen so his lips won't move,

A BOAT: Adjective or Adverb, we have a hard time telling the difference: Canadian ice fishing term as in, "I think I'm a-boat to freeze to death."

BAIT: Noun: The highest and best use for the leftovers from the time your sister-in-law tried a new casserole and no one could choke it down. Also, see "Sushi."

BASS: Noun: A singer with a low voice. Also a type of fish that lurks down under dead trees and debris, sometimes nesting down there, but which, under normal circumstances, will never be mistaken for a chicken. Why these two words are both spelled the same is one of the great mysteries of the English language.

BITE: Verb: The thing the deer flies and mosquitoes always do, but which the fish sometimes don't do, one taking place on the back of your neck and exposed arms, the other not taking place on your hook.

CARP: Noun: The only fish I know that you can catch first thing in the morning, let him rest on the ground all day long in the hot sun, and then wait until the evening to throw him back after he looks more like a baseball glove than a fish, and there is still a pretty good chance he will survive to reproduce.

Verb: What your spouse does at you sometimes when she would rather have you stay home and clean the oil spot off from the driveway instead of going fishing.

CAST: Noun: The thing your doctor puts on your leg after your buddy tries to help you land the big one by backing up the boat which takes the propeller into your line shredding it, so out of frustration you kick the cooler breaking your metacarpals.

CAT FISH: Noun: The fish you caught after using a gunnysack full of cats to chum or for bait as described in earlier chapters.

CRAPPIE: A fish that looks like a road pizza even without being run over.

CREEL: Noun: A place to put your fish on good days and on the other days, your sandwich.

DRY FLY: Noun: A fly, which on your back swing as you cast, wraps itself around the tree branches behind you and never makes it to the water.

FISH FINDER: Noun: Fisherman not far from you who is having a great time catching fish while you are being skunked.

FLOAT TUBE: Noun: A complicated device designed to gradually leak water until a fisherman's toes are numb as it drifts toward the shore far from where the fisherman wants to be.

HALIBUT: Noun: A fish which is about as much fun to land as a rock or old car, but which tastes pretty good for something with both eyes on the same side of it's head.

JIG: Noun: The dance you do when you're putting bait on your hook and someone walks through your line causing the hook to stick into your thumb.

LEADER: Adjective: The amount of booze it takes to stay warm for two hours ice fishing.

LIMIT: The number of times a guy can skip work or important honey-do jobs and sneak off with his buddies to go fishing before he finds his desk emptied out or the locks changed and his clothes thrown out in the street when he comes home.

LINE: Verb: What a fisherman is usually doing when is lips are moving.

LURE: Noun: Hundreds of worthless metal objects (that the guy at the sporting goods store talks you into buying against your better judgement) that are guaranteed to take money from fishermen, while not necessarily impressing the fish.

MARSHMALLOW: Noun: One of the only substances, which can legitimately double as bait for the fish, and food for the fisherman in times of need.

MINNOW: Noun: A term used to describe the fish you caught which you choose to refer to as "pan sized," and which rival fishermen would describe as "bait."

NET: Noun: A device used to help land fish, and in an emergency to skim the leaves out of the pancake batter when you're cooking outside in the wind.

NIBBLE: Verb: The thing you do to your sandwiches in order to salvage what you can by eating around the edges when you are starving, having fished all day long without taking time to eat anything except for liquids, and since you weren't thinking when you put your lunch box on the floor of the boat, periodically, throughout the day water seeped in soaking the food in there with some pretty nasty slime-water.

PERCH: Verb: The thing you do outside in a bush, tree, or on the front porch until morning because you got home so late your wife locked the doors on you.

PROCLAMATION: Noun: A statement made by a fisherman when fishing has been lousy so far and so he changes his bait so now he thinks he will start catching them. An Example of a proclamation: "No fish will be able to resist this beauty; I'm finally ready to start catching 'em."

RELEASE: Verb: Having had a pretty good time after spending a week on a houseboat with friends, many people will "re-lease" the boat to try and do it again.

SARDINE: Noun: A triple threat, this material can be used as the meat for your sandwich, as bait when you forget to buy some, or, you can take them home and pretend you caught them if you get skunked and have a compelling need to prove you actually went fishing.

SINKER: Verb: What you do to your boat when you're in the middle of the lake and you discover you forgot to put the drain plug back in 'er, which allows water to come in faster than you can bail 'er out with your coffee can.

SKUNKED: Verb: What happens when the sun goes down and you are slaying them, and so you don't want to stop fishing until finally it gets too dark to see as you walk around the lake, and since you can't see the trail you also can't see the skunk, and so you step on it. The skunk then sprays you from head to toe.

SPINNER: Verb: The thing you do with an empty beverage container when you're up at the lake and it rains and lightnings the whole time and so you're bored and sitting at the table staring out the window wishing you were fishing .

STEELHEAD: Noun: The kind of head you wish you had instead of the one connected to your neck the morning after you and your buddies drank all the booze you took on your last fishing trip.

TACKLE: Verb: The thing you do to the guy who got to the lake a few seconds ahead of you, and who looks like he's about to start fishing in your favorite spot.

TROPHY: Noun: An extraordinarily large fish which never seems to get caught, but which shows the fisherman just a tiny glimpse of itself before breaking the line and swimming away, which forces the fisherman to fill in the gaps using his imagination when describing the fish to others.

WADERS: Nouns: Fishermen who can't afford a boat.

WET FLY: Noun: Any one of the flies stuck on your hat when you slip while crossing the stream causing you to fall in headfirst.

WHOPPER: Verb: What you do to your old Evinrude motor to finally get 'er to kick over after she's been in the garage since last fall.

WORM: Noun: This is a type of animal which normally looks revolting, but I'll bet if a guy were to wrap a few of them around the outside of a piece of cork or bread or something and then place them on a plate of Sushi, I'll bet somebody would eat it.

ZERO: Adjective: The number of fish you caught on the flies you tied yourself the first month or so after you got your fly tying set for Christmas, before you started buying them from the bait shop and lying about tying them yourself.

Order these additional Apricot Press Books

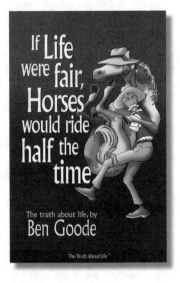

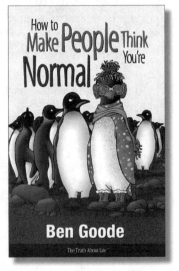

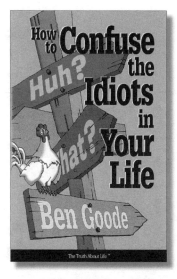
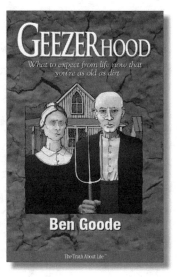
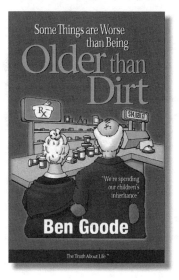
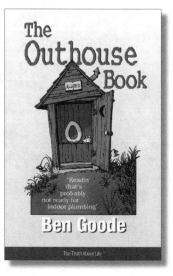

Order these additional Apricot Press Books

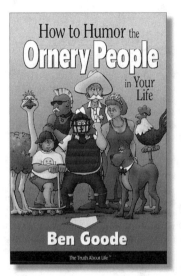

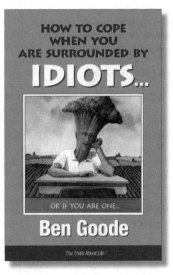

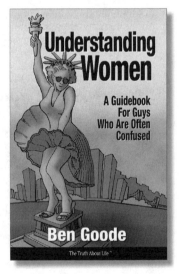

Order Online! www.apricotpress.com

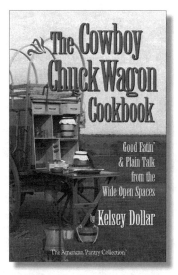

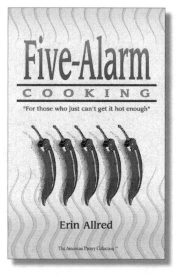

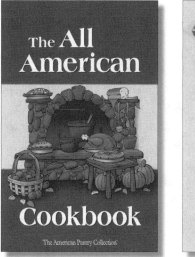

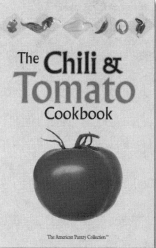

Order these additional Apricot Press Books

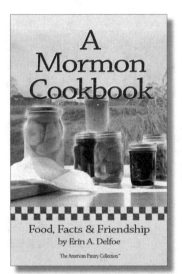

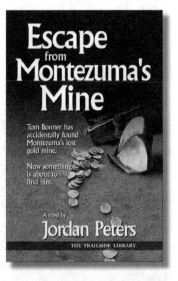

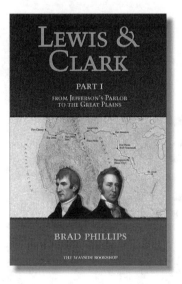

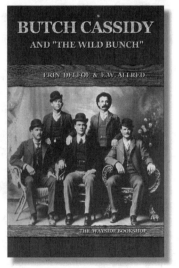

Order Online! www.apricotpress.com

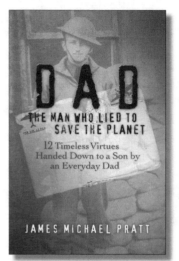

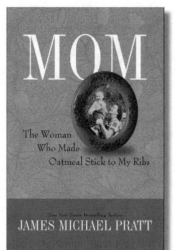